EMOTIONS and FEELINGS

Guilt

Sarah Harvey

Explore other books at:
WWW.ENGAGEBOOKS.COM

VANCOUVER, B.C.

e → WWW.ENGAGEBOOKS.COM

Guilt: Level 2
Emotions and Feelings
Harvey, Sarah N. 1950 –
Text © 2023 Engage Books
Design © 2023 Engage Books

Edited by: A.R. Roumanis, Ashley Lee, Melody Sun,
and Sarah Harvey
Design by: Mandy Christiansen

Text set in Arial Regular.
Chapter headings set in Arial Black.

FIRST EDITION / FIRST PRINTING

LIBRARY AND ARCHIVES CANADA CATALOGUING IN PUBLICATION

Title: Guilt / Sarah Harvey.
Names: Harvey, Sarah N., 1950- author.
Description: Series statement: Emotions and feelings

Identifiers: Canadiana (print) 20230447317 | Canadiana (ebook) 20230447325
ISBN 978-1-77878-160-5 (hardcover)
ISBN 978-1-77878-161-2 (softcover)
ISBN 978-1-77878-162-9 (epub)
ISBN 978-1-77878-163-6 (pdf)
ISBN 978-1-77878-164-3 (audio)

Subjects:
LCSH: Guilt—Juvenile literature.
LCSH: Guilt in children—Juvenile literature.

Classification: LCC BF723.G83 H37 2023 | DDC J155.4/1244—DC23

This project has been made possible in part
by the Government of Canada.

Canada 🍁

Contents

What Is Guilt?

Guilt is an **emotion**. It happens when you think you have done something wrong.

KEY WORD

Emotion: a strong feeling.

4

Guilt is part of your moral code. This is your own sense of what is right and wrong.

Guilt can be a big feeling or a small one.

Why Do People Feel Guilty?

People feel guilty for many reasons. You can feel guilty about not doing something you meant to do.

You may feel guilty if you forgot to do your homework.

You can also feel guilty about doing something you did not mean to do. Knocking over a cup of water by mistake can make you feel guilty.

Are There Different Kinds of Guilt?

There are two main kinds of guilt. Healthy guilt is when you know you did something wrong.

Healthy guilt helps people learn from their mistakes.

You cannot control how other people feel.

Unhealthy guilt is when you did not do anything wrong but you feel like you did. It may be your turn to pick a family movie. If you pick something your brother does not like, you may feel guilty.

How Does Guilt Affect the Way You Think?

Guilt can take over your mind. You may not stop thinking about what you did. You may think everyone is mad at you.

Talk to an adult if you are feeling shame.

When you feel bad, you may think you are bad. This is called shame.

How Does Guilt Affect the Way You Act?

Guilt can make you want to be alone. You might cry a lot. You may get angry at people you love.

Sometimes people will lie about what they have done. They may act as if nothing has happened.

People who lie are often afraid of what people will think of them.

Can Guilt Ever Be a Good Thing?

Guilt can be a good thing. It helps people learn from their mistakes. It can make people change the way they act.

Feeling guilt means you know what is right and wrong. It helps you do the right thing.

Does Everyone Feel Guilt?

Guilt is a normal feeling for most people. Everyone does something wrong once in a while.

Some people feel guilty more often than others. They think they are the cause of everyone's problems.

Ask an adult for help if you feel guilty a lot.

What Does Guilt Feel Like?

Guilt can make you feel sad and afraid. Many people say that they feel as if they are carrying a big **burden**.

KEY WORD

Burden: a heavy load.

Guilt can cause you to feel many things in your body.
- Stomach pain and upset
- Headaches
- Extreme tiredness
- Racing heart
- Not wanting to eat
- Problems sleeping

19

Can You Stop Guilt From Happening?

There is no way to stop guilt from happening. Everyone makes mistakes. You can make yourself feel better by **making amends**.

KEY WORD

Making amends: doing things to show you are sorry about something you have done.

You can try to **ignore** feelings of guilt. This is not healthy. It can make things worse for you and the person that you hurt.

Does Guilt Change as You Grow Older?

As people get older, they often learn how to deal with guilt in a healthy way. Not everybody tries to do this.

People learn to think more about other people's feelings as they get older. This can stop them from making mistakes that will make them feel guilty.

Does Guilt Ever Go Away?

Healthy guilt does not usually last long. It goes away if you make amends and change the way you behave.

Unhealthy guilt can last longer. You often have to change the way you think instead of making amends.

What Can You Do if You Are Feeling Guilty?

Make sure you know why you feel guilty. If you are not sure of the reason, try talking with an adult.

If you know why you feel guilty, try to fix your mistake. If it cannot be fixed, say sorry to the person you hurt.

What Can You Do if Someone Else Is Feeling Guilty?

If someone you know feels guilty, listen to them. They may just need someone to talk to about their problems.

Help your friend come up with a plan to fix their mistakes. They will feel better if they make amends.

Quiz

Test your knowledge of guilt by answering the following questions. The questions are based on what you have read in this book. The answers are listed on the bottom of the next page.

1 What is your moral code?

2 What are the two main types of guilt?

3 Can you control how other people feel?

4 How can you make yourself feel better?

5 Which kind of guilt lasts longer?

6 What should you do if someone you know feels guilty?

Explore other books in the Emotions and Feelings series.

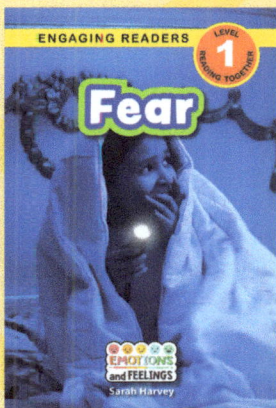

Visit www.engagebooks.com/readers

Answers: 1. Your own sense of what is right and wrong 2. Healthy guilt and unhealthy guilt 3. No 4. By making amends 5. Unhealthy guilt 6. Listen to them

www.ingramcontent.com/pod-product-compliance
Lightning Source LLC
Chambersburg PA
CBHW051236020426
42331CB00016B/3407